**Oxford
Reading
Tree**

D1740650

Copymasters Book 1

THELMA PAGE   SUE PALMER

OXFORD

OXFORD
UNIVERSITY PRESS

Great Clarendon Street, Oxford OX2 6DP

Oxford University Press is a department of the University of Oxford. It furthers the University's objective of excellence in research, scholarship, and education by publishing worldwide in

Oxford   New York

Athens Auckland Bangkok Bogotá Buenos Aires Calcutta
Cape Town Chenna Dar es Salaam Delhi Florence Hong Kong
Istanbul Karachi Kuala Lumpur Madrid Melbourne Mexico City
Mumbai Nairobi Paris São Paulo Singapore Taipei Tokyo
Toronto Warsaw

with associated companies in Berlin Ibadan

Oxford is a registered trade mark of Oxford University Press in the UK and in certain other countries

Published in the United States by Oxford University Press Inc., New York

The Magic Key is a trade mark of HIT Entertainment PLC

Text and illustrations copyright Oxford University Press 2000
Storylines copyright Oxford Publishing Limited, Roderick Hunt, Alex Brychta, and HIT Entertainment PLC 2000

The moral rights of the authors have been asserted
Database right Oxford University Press (maker)

First published 2000

British Library Cataloguing in Publication Data

Data available

ISBN 0 19 919361 4

www.oup.co.uk/primary

Front cover artwork courtesy of HIT Entertainment PLC

Illustrated by Jan and Alex Brychta

Printed in the UK by Progressive Printng Ltd.

The Magic Key Copymasters Book 1 is based on the television series The Magic Key, produced by HIT Entertainment PLC for BBC School Television.

Contents

* *Note:* All teaching objectives relate to Year 1 Term 1.

Introduction

Each programme in the BBC series, *The Magic Key*, an animated version of the *Oxford Reading Tree* by Roderick Hunt and Alex Brychta, is planned around particular teaching objectives from the National Literacy Strategy. For example, Programme 1 introduces and practises the use of full stops. For the complete list, see Contents (pages 2–3).

The copymasters provide activities to follow up the teaching objectives introduced by the television programmes. For each programme there are six sheets reinforcing the main teaching objectives and enabling children to practise other skills from Year 1 Term 1.

While some of the activities use the context, characters or situations from the programmes, the emphasis is always on the teaching objectives. Instead of using the more complex vocabulary of the programmes, the copymasters are based on:
- high frequency words from the NLS Reception word list;
- words that Year 1 children should be able to decode;
- familiar *Oxford Reading Tree* names, and words which are easily cued by pictures.

As well as reinforcing the main objectives for each programme, the activities also provide opportunities for practice of such skills as alphabetical order, blending CVC words and generating rhyming words. There are also a number of games included, to add variety.

How to use the copymasters

Most activities are self-explanatory, but where further information is necessary it is included in a note to the teacher, in small print at the base of the sheet.

Many of the copymasters are in pairs, involving similar activities, and may be used to provide differentiated follow up:
- Enlarge the first copymaster of a pair, and use as a shared activity.
- Differentiate by a) asking less able children to try the same copymaster, modelling their work on your demonstration; b) giving more able children the second copymaster to complete independently.

Paired copymasters may also be used to provide extra practice for those children who need more than one try at an activity, or for revision of a particular skill at a later date.

1. Full stops

Name: .... Date: ....

Cut out the labels and stick them on the right kennels.
Put in the full stops.

| Floppy is asleep | Floppy likes his bone |
| Floppy and Biff like to play | Floppy is on top |

1. Full stops

Name: .... Date: ....

Cut out the labels and stick them on the right kennels.
Put in the full stops.

| The cat is on top | Floppy can see the cat |
| The cat runs away | Floppy tells the cat to go away |

Y1T1: S5/S8/T12

1. Full stops

Name: .... Date: ....

Put the full stops in the speech bubbles.

Write the sentences on the sign.

Show where each ends with a full stop.

Teacher's Notes
Ensure pupils understand that a sentence ends with a full stop and
not necessarily at the end of a line.

1. Full stops

Name: .... Date: ....

Put the full stops in the speech bubbles.

This is for Floppy

It is a big bone

Write the sentences on the label.

Show where each sentence ends with a full stop.

Teacher's Notes
Ensure pupils understand that a sentence ends with a full stop and
not necessarily at the end of a line.

Y1T1: S5/S6/S7/S8

Name: .... **Date:** ....

Cut out the chocolate bars and divide them up.

Make sentences about the picture.

| box | a | . | Kipper | has |

| digs | . | hole | a | Chip |

| Wilf | Floppy | with | . | sits |

Teacher's Notes
(Optional) Pupils could write the sentences on a piece of paper.

1. Full stops

Name: .... **Date:** ....

Cut out the chocolate bars and divide them up.

Make sentences about the pictures.

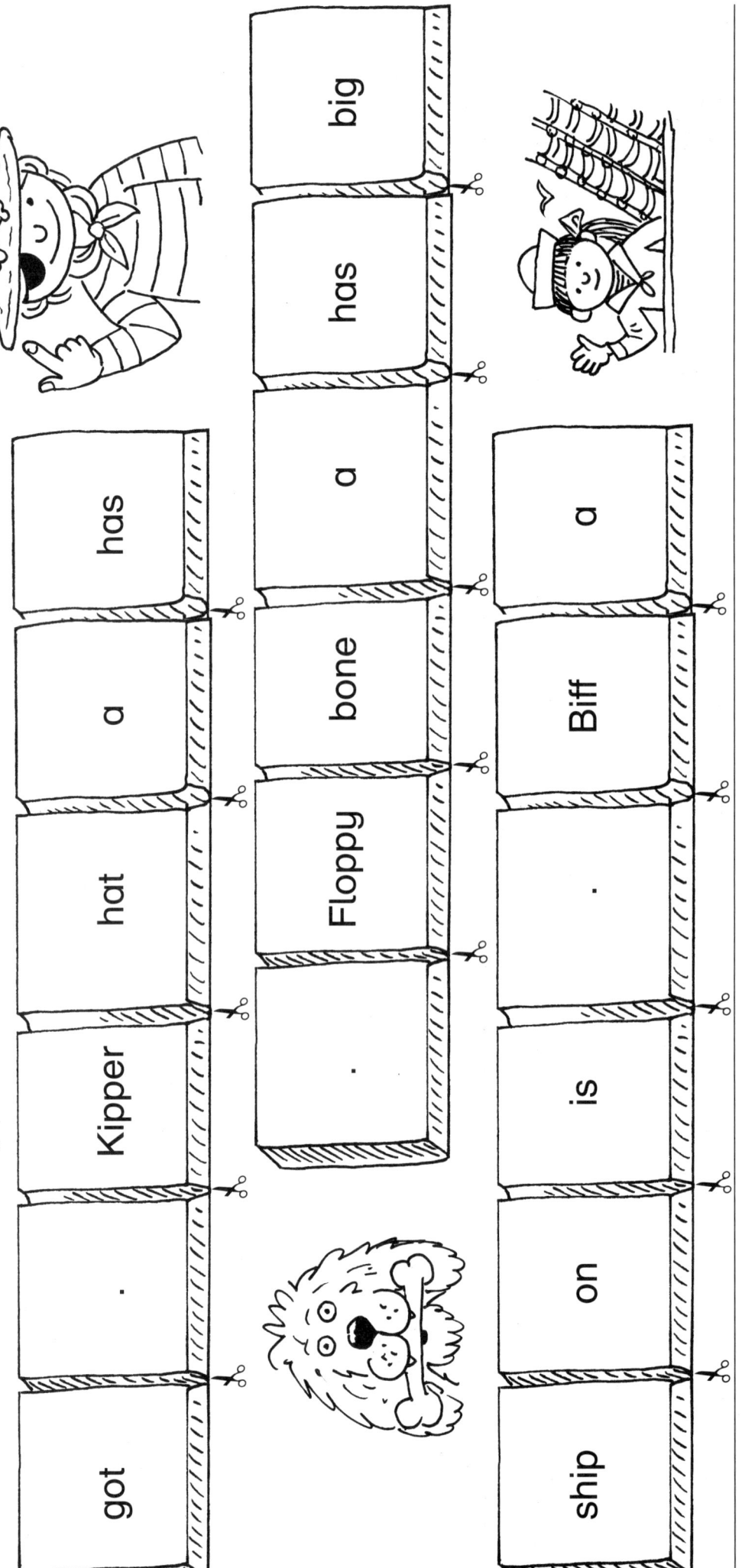

got . Kipper hat a has

. Floppy bone a has big

ship on is . Biff a

Teacher's Notes
(Optional) Pupils could write the sentences on a piece of paper.

2. Capital letters   Name: ....   Date: ....

A B C D E F G H I J K L M

Write the names of the shops in capital letters.

corner shop   toy shop

Copy the alphabet.

N O P Q R S T U V W X Y Z

2. Capital letters

Name: .... Date: ....

Write the missing letters in the names.

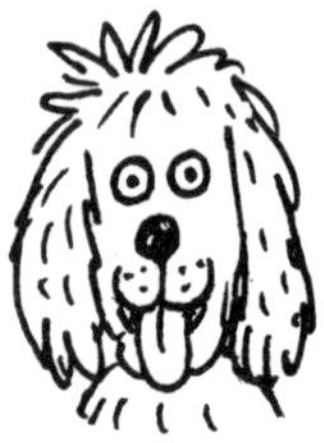

I am ....loppy.

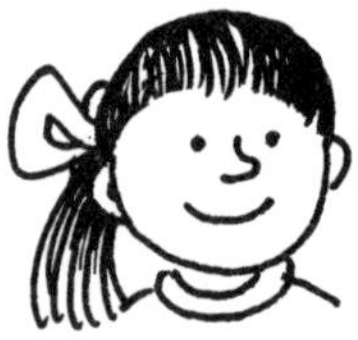

I am ....iff.

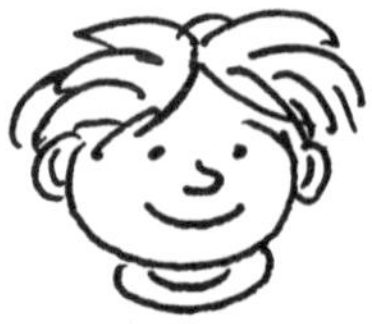

I am ....ipper.

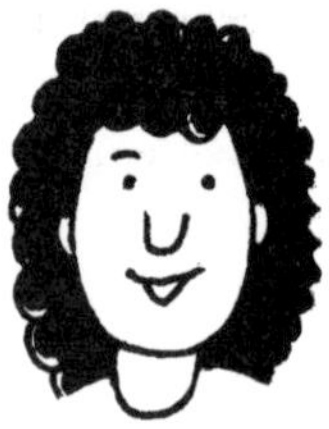

I am ....ilma.

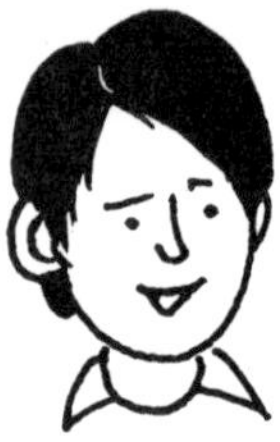

I am ....adim.

| F |
| B |
| W |
| N |
| K |

Who are you?

Draw yourself and write the sentence.

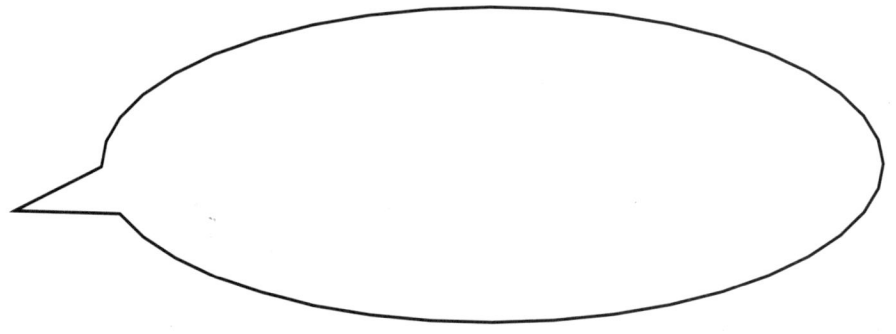

2. Capital letters

Name: .... Date: ....

Use letters on the mug to make rhyming words.

MUG

Use letters on the bin to make rhyming words.

BIN

----

2. Capital letters

Name: ....

Date: ....

Trace the letters, then finish the letter patterns.

H I H I H I

E F E F E F

A V A V A V

X Y X Y X Y

Z T Z T Z T

2. Capital letters

Names: ....

Date: ....

☐ ☐

A →	B	C	D	E	F	G	H	I →
Z	Y	X	W	V	U	T	S	R	Q	P	O	N ↓

(game board with flowers containing lower-case letters a–z arranged in a track)

Teacher's Notes

Instructions:

1. Play in pairs. Each person needs a coloured pencil, a counter, and a dice to share.
2. Colour the box by your name.
3. Starting at A, take turns to throw the dice and travel around the track.
4. When you land on a letter, find and colour the equivalent lower case letter. Each flower can only be coloured in once.
5. Go round the track twice. The winner is the player with most flowers in his or her colour.

Y1T1: S5/W2

15

2:5

2. Capital letters

Name: .... Date: ....

Glue here.

A	B	C		E	F			
a		d		g	h	i		

Glue here.

J		L					Q	
			n	o		r		

S					X			
		u	v		z			

Teacher's Notes

Instructions:

1. Fill in the missing letters in the alphabet.
2. Cut out and glue strips together.
   Children could work on this at home.

3. Capital 'I'

Name: .... Date: ....

Write 'I' in the labels.

Cut out the labels and stick them in the right speech bubbles.

... 'm cold.

... am the best.

... 'm wet.

... 'm muddy.

3. Capital 'I'

Name: .... Date: ....

Write 'I' in the labels.

Cut out the labels and stick them in the right speech bubbles.

| ... can play. | ... can run. |
| ... wag my tail. | ... like bones. |

Y1T1: S4/S9

3. Capital 'I'

Name: .... Date: ....

I am a ....

gorilla

scarecrow

....

knight

cat

....

3. Capital 'I'

Name: .... Date: ....

I am a _____

bat

duck

_____

_____

dog

fish

_____

Y1T1: S8/S9/T14

Start here

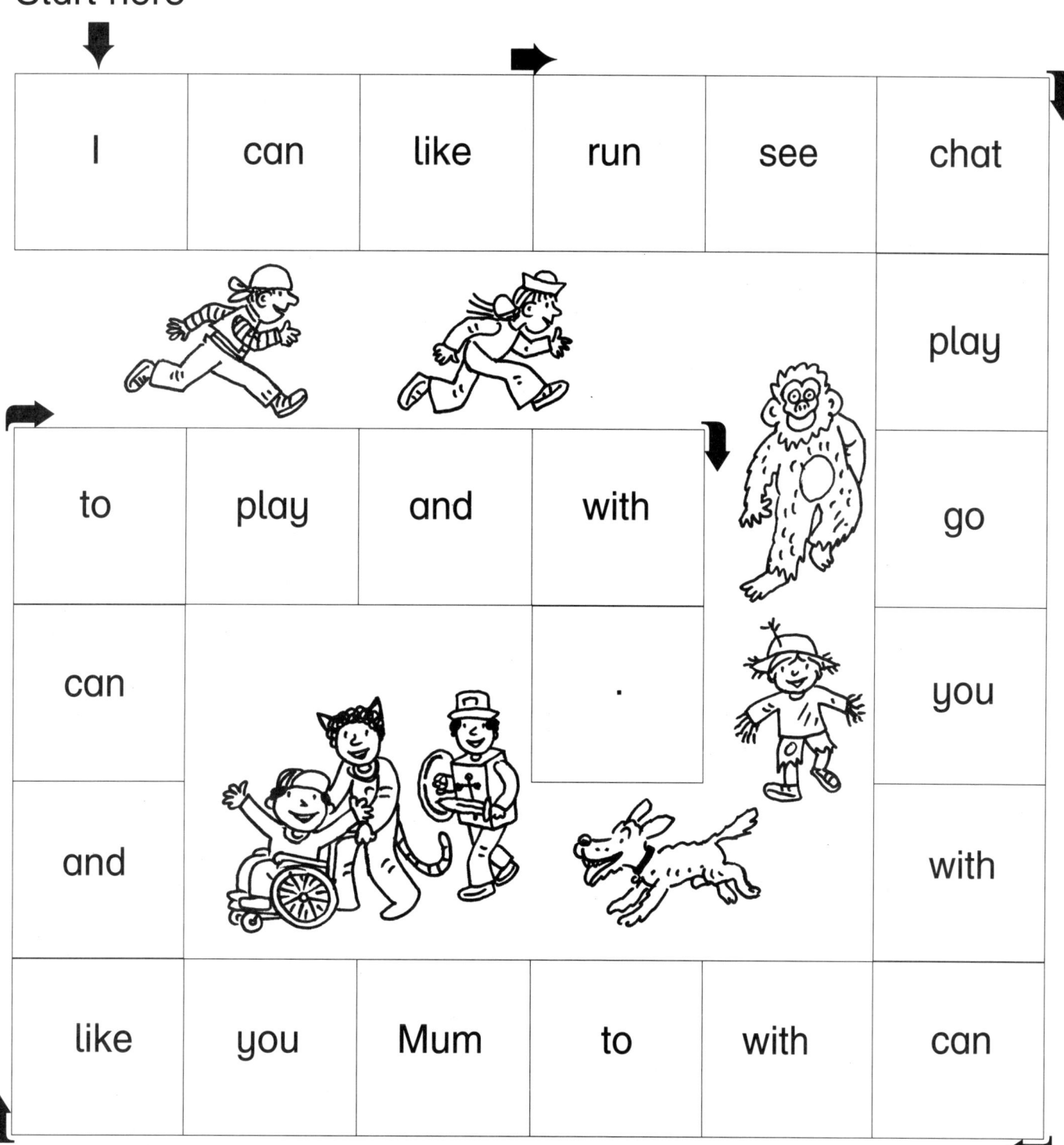

I	can	like	run	see	chat

to	play	and	with		go
can			.		you
and					with
like	you	Mum	to	with	can

Teacher's Notes

This is a game for pairs. Each pair will need a dice.

Each child will need a counter, a pencil and a record sheet (PCM 3.6).

See PCM 3.6 for full instructions.

Record sheets

Name: ----------------------------

I ----------------------------

Name: ----------------------------

I ----------------------------

Teacher's Notes

Instructions:

1. Take turns to throw the dice to see how many squares to move.
2. Write the words you land on, on your record sheet.
3. Throw the correct number to get a full stop at the end.
4. When you have got your full stop, use some of your words to make a sentence.
5. The winner is the one who makes the longest sentence. (It must make sense!)

4. Short sentences

Name: .... Date: ....

Use the words to make sentences.

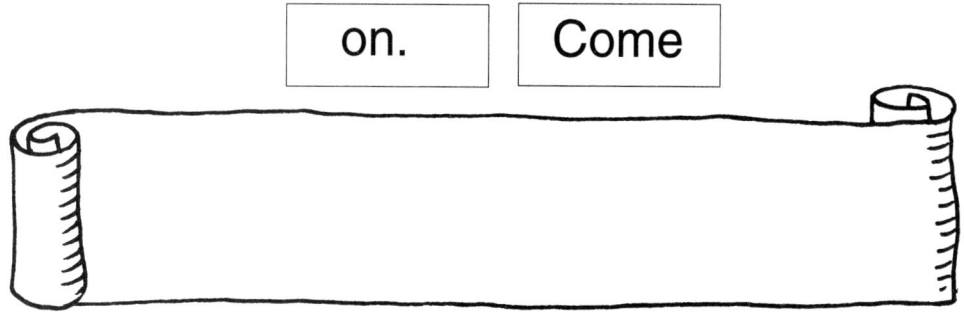

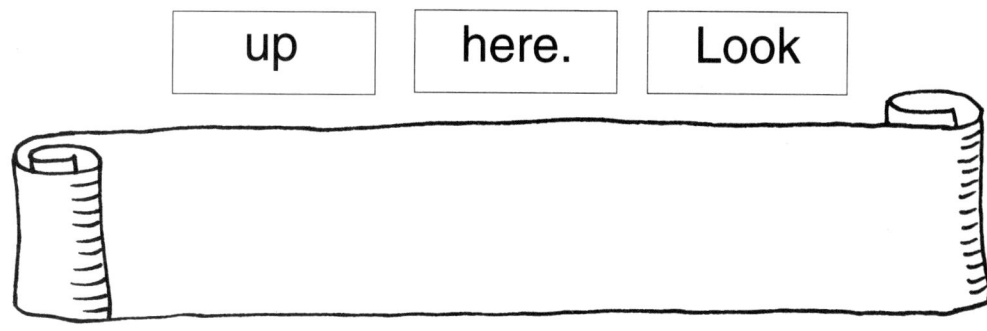

Make up another sentence.

4. Short sentences

Name: .... Date: ....

Cut out the words and make 3 sentences.

1. ....

2. ....

3. ....

Mum	Biff's	We	like	.
Dad	get	.	said	in
away	Floppy	went	.	

4. Short sentences

Name: .... Date: ....

Count the letters in each word.
Write the word on the right balloon.

a

cat

come

in

I

and

can

is

like

to

play

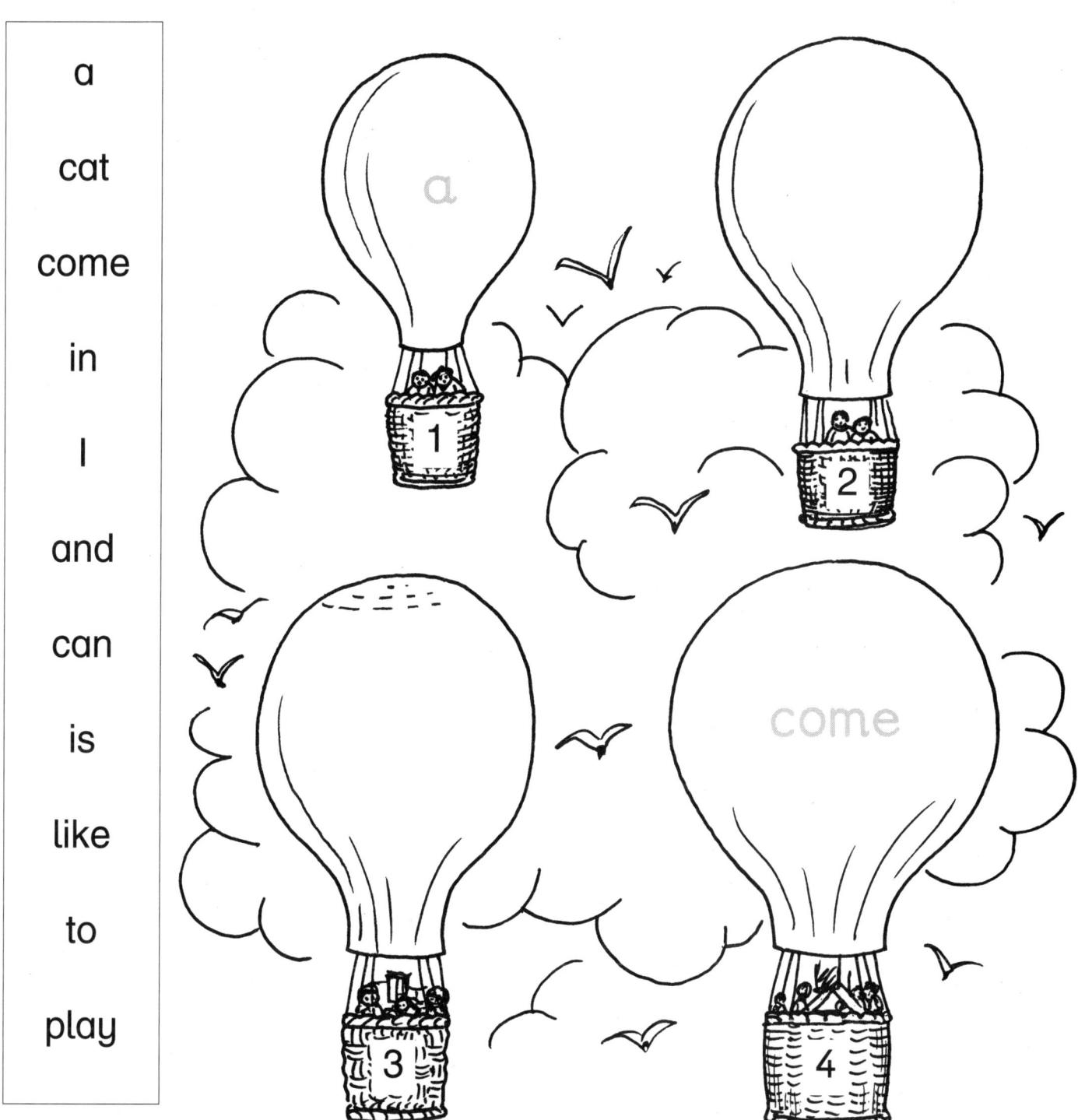

Use some of the words to write a sentence.

....

4. Short sentences

Names: .... ☐ Date: ....

....☐

a	b	c	d	e	f
z	all am big can cat				g
y	day for get go he				h
x	is it like look Mum				i
w					j
v	my no of on play				k
u	said they to up				l
t	was went yes you				m
s	r	q	p	o	n

Teacher's Notes

Instructions:

1. Play in pairs. Each person has one counter and a coloured pencil. Colour the squares by your names.
2. Starting at 'a', take turns to throw the dice and move along the track.
3. When you land on a letter, find a word beginning with that letter and cross it out in your colour. If there is no word beginning with that letter, throw again.
4. Use the words crossed out in your colour to make the longest sentence you can.
5. The winner is the player who makes the longest sentence.

4. Short sentences

Name: .... Date: ....

Choose letters from the balloons to write the words.

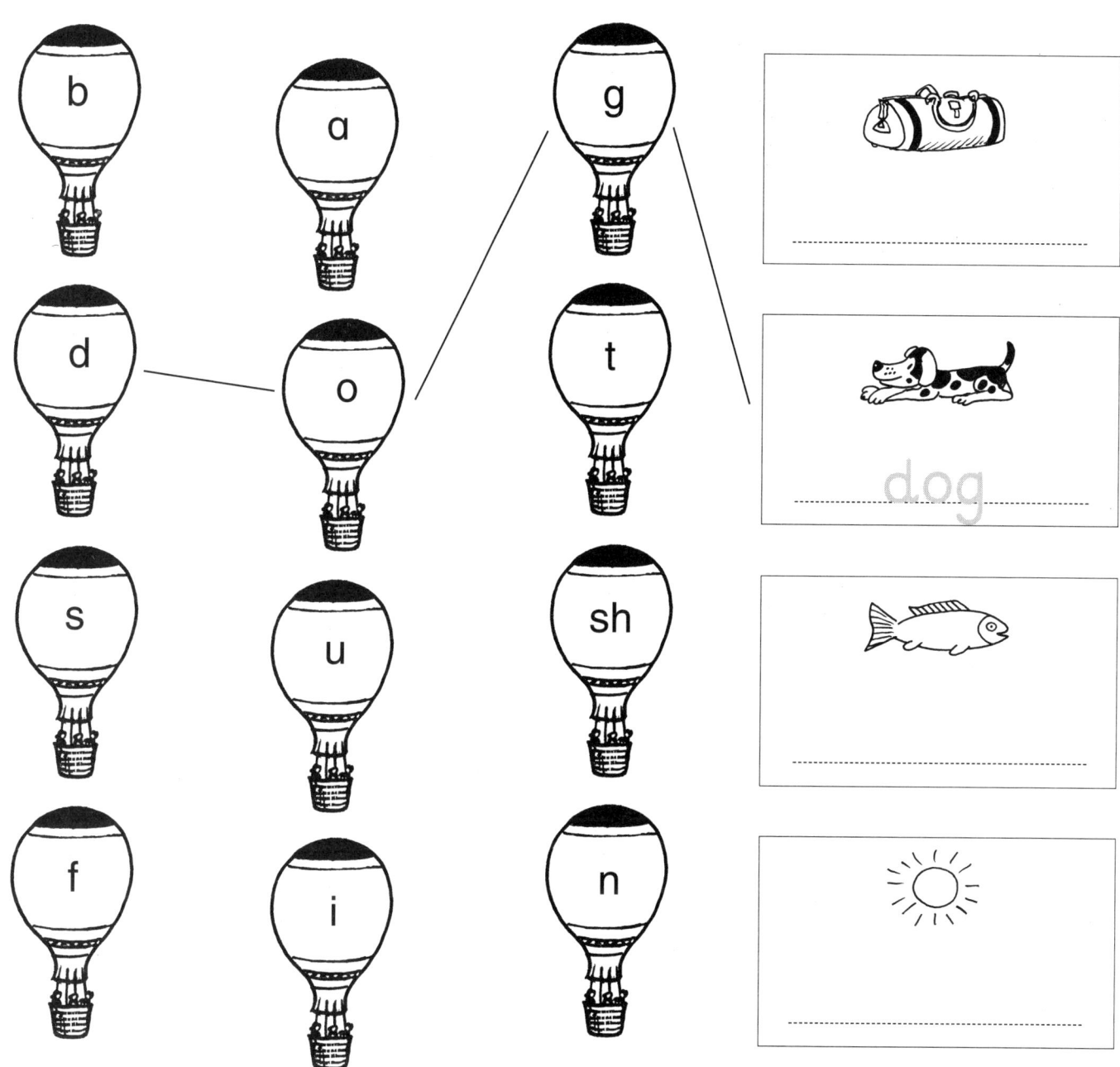

Use 3 of the words in sentences.

1. ....

2. ....

3. ....

4. Short sentences

Name: .... Date: ....

Put in the full stops.

Gran is in the balloon

Biff and Nadim are in the balloon

The balloon is going up

Write the sentences by the pictures.

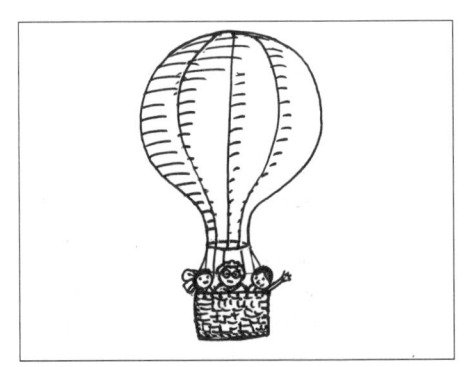

Y1T1: S6/S8/S9

Name: .... Date: ....

✽ Once upon a time there was a dog.

✹ It was sad.

✽ The dog saw a bone.

✹ It was happy!

✽ A troll took the bone.

✹ The dog got the bone and ran away.

✽ The troll was sad!

✹ The dog came back.

✽ ✹ They all lived happily ever after.

Teacher's Notes

Instructions:
1. Work with a partner. One is ✹ and the other is ✽.
2. Read the lines with your symbol. Use the right expression.
3. Swap over symbols and try it again, improving your expression.
4. (Optional) Read into a tape-recorder. Then play back to hear your expression.

Y1T1: W9/S2/S3/T2

5. Reading with expression

Name: .... Date: ....

✻ Once upon a time there was a teddy.

❁ He was sad.

✻ The teddy saw a big carrot.

❁ He was happy!

✻ A troll took the carrot.

❁ The teddy got the carrot and ran away.

✻ The troll was sad!

❁ The teddy came back.

✻ ❁ They all lived happily ever after.

Teacher's Notes
This PCM is suitable for children who need more practice of key
vocabulary. It uses the same language structures and most of the
same words as PCM 5.1 .
Use the same instructions as for PCM 5.1.

Name: .... Date: ....

1.

I can see a big troll.

2.

Who said that?

3.

Me.

Get back, Gran!

4.

Get Gran! *Help!*

5.

I have got you.

Stop! Put me down.

6.

Oh no! They have got Gran!

Teacher's Notes

Instructions:

1. Work with a partner. One person says what is happening in each picture. Then the
   other reads the speech bubbles in the right voices, with lots of expression.
2. Swap over and tell/read again.

Name: .... Date: ....

1.

Put her in the pot.

No!

2.

Who said that?

I did!

3.

Put potatoes in the pot.

Yum!

4.

Put frogs in the pot.

Yuck!

5.

Put carrots in the pot.

Yum!

6.

Mmmm! It *is* good!

Teacher's Notes

Instructions:

1. Work with a partner. One person says what is happening in each picture. Then the other reads the speech bubbles in the right voices, with lots of expression.
2. Swap over and tell/read again.

5. Reading with expression

Name: .... Date: ....

Start here

Put the cards

from PCM 5.6

here –

face down.

Teacher's Notes

Instructions:

1. Cut out cards on PCM 5.6 to play the game.
2. Each player needs a counter and a shared dice.
3. Take turns to throw the dice to see how many squares you move.
4. When you land on a square, pick up a card.

5. Read the words on your card with the right voice and expression for the person on your square.
6. Continue the game until all the cards have been used.

5. Reading with expression

I like you.	It is bed time.	May I have a drink?
Help!	I am happy.	I will get you!
This is not fun.	I am sad.	Run! Run away!
This is fun.	Oh no!	It is fun to play this.

Teacher's Notes
Cut out the cards to use with the game on PCM 5.5.

6. Sentences making sense

Name: .... Date: ....

Cut out the puzzle.

Make the sentence.

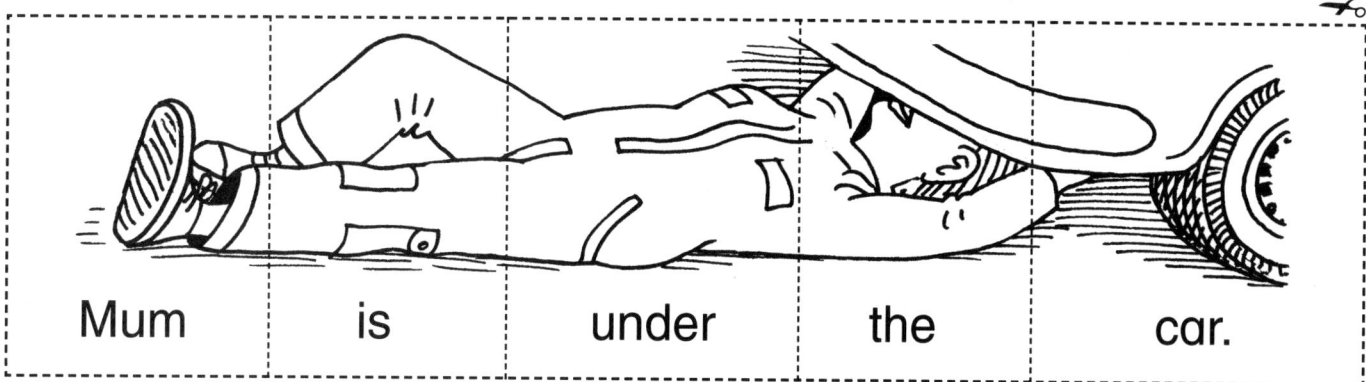

| Mum | is | under | the | car. |

Draw the picture.

Cut out the puzzle.

| A | cat | is | in | the | tree. |

Teacher's Notes

Extension:
1. Make your own puzzle by writing a sentence and drawing a picture.
2. Cut it up then ask a friend to make the puzzle.

---

6. Sentences making sense

Name: .... Date: ....

Write Floppy's sentences.
Put in full stops.

I can ....

I ....

....

....

eat   chase my tail   bark   sniff

Write one more sentence about Floppy.

....

6. Sentences making sense

Name: .... Date: ....

Join the beginning and end of each sentence.

| Anneena was |

| her Mum. |

| It was for |

| making a patchwork. |

| It was a |

| help Anneena. |

| Chip wanted to |

| picture of a cat. |

Use one of the endings to finish this sentence.

Floppy liked the ....

Name: .... Date: ....

are · is · me · big · this

I · see · this

going · Kipper · can

looked · am

went · home · house

played · a

we · Chip · cats

dog · liked

My words ....

My sentence ....

Teacher's Notes

Instructions:

1. Each player needs a copy of the game and a pencil.
2. Use one dice, taking turns to throw it and choose a word with that number of letters.
3. Draw a ring around the word and write it at the bottom of the page.
4. When you have at least 3 words, try making them into a sentence, remembering a capital letter and a full stop.

5. Continue throwing the dice for new words until you can make a sentence.
6. The winner is the first player who makes a sentence.
(Extension) The winner is the first player to write 3 sentences with at least 3 words in each. (Pupils may need to use the back of the sheet to complete this game.)

6. Sentences making sense

Name: .... Date: ....

Read the sentences.

Draw a pin person over the extra word.

Write the sentence.

He can not get was down.

He can not get down.

The door in is at the top.

The fish are on the three road.

Anneena went to see for the patchworker.

___

Teacher's Notes

Extension

1. Make up a sentence and put in an extra word. Write it on the back of the sheet.
2. Ask a friend to cross out the extra word.

___

Y1T1: S1

6. Sentences making sense

Name: .... Date: ....

Join the fish to make sentences.

Write your sentences here.

Anneena was on the ship.

Y1T1: S1/S6/S8

7. Working out new words

Name: .... Date: ....

Use the pictures to guess the missing words.
Draw a line from the picture to the right word.

Wilma and Wilf went to see the  . He

crown

king

sat on a  . He had a  .

throne

Wilma told the  that she had a  . It

message

king

was from the  across the  .

river

people

Wilma said that the  across the

river

people

 would  . The  was

king

fight

sad. He liked the  .

people

7. Working out new words

Name: .... Date: ....

Fill in the missing words from the boxes.

dance	river	trees

Wilma and Wilf dressed up like 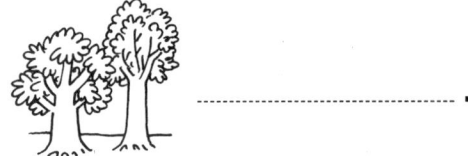 ....

They crossed the  .... They saw the

people  ....

dance	king	happy	fight	danced

Wilma saw that the people wanted to  .... not

 .... She ran to tell the  ....

The king was happy. They all  .... They

were  ....

Y1T1: S1/S2/T2

7. Working out new words

Name: .... Date: ....

Fill in the missing letters.
Use the words in the boxes to help you.

This is F _____ . He is a b ____ dog. Floppy

likes b _____ . He has a k _____ .

big

kennel

He likes to go to s _____ in his kennel.

Floppy

sleep

bones

This is K _____ . He is not v _____ big. He

has a t _____ . Kipper l _____ his teddy.

teddy

Kipper

loves

very

Teacher's Notes
1. Work in pairs.
2. Read a sentence each. Help each other work out the missing
   words. Talk about how you work them out.

Name: .... Date: ....

Read the message then write it out.

was   .

was lost.

At   Kipper went to the   .

He found   .

was   .

----

7. Working out new words

Biff was _____ .

The sun was in the _____ .

This woman is a _____ .

Kipper was _____ .

The _____ was in the tree.

A _____ sat on the mat.

Teacher's Notes

Instructions:
1. Copy PCMs 7.5 and 7.6 onto card.
2. Cut out the sentence strips and place face down in a pile.
3. Cut out the word cards, shuffle and place face down in another pile.

4. Take turns to take a strip, read it, turn over the word cards, until you find one that fits.
5. Everyone must agree on the word choice, before moving on to the next sentence.

There were six candles on the _____ .

The dog _____ at the man.

Nadim _____ on his computer.

Put the _____ in the cup.

cat	cake	barked	played	milk
hot	sky	vet	cold	bird

Teacher's Notes
See PCM 7.5 for instructions.

Y1T1: S1/S2/T2

8. Labels

Name: .... Date: ....

Look at the first phoneme of each word.
Match the labels to the pictures.
Write new labels.

| banana |

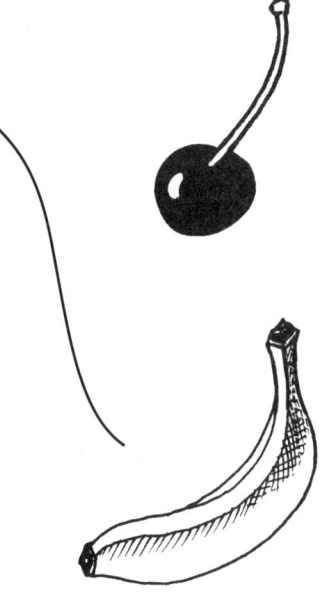

| cherry |

banana

| apple |

| strawberry |

| orange |

Y1T1: W12/T2 47

8. Labels

Name: .... Date: ....

Write secret labels for the jars.

Use your secret bottles to make a spell.

Mix together:

2 drops of

.... drops of ....

1 jar of .... and ....

This will make a ....

....

8. Labels

Name: .... Date: ....

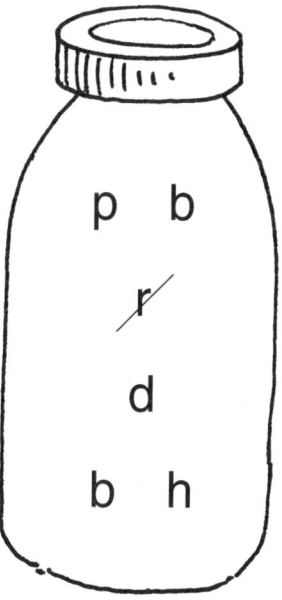
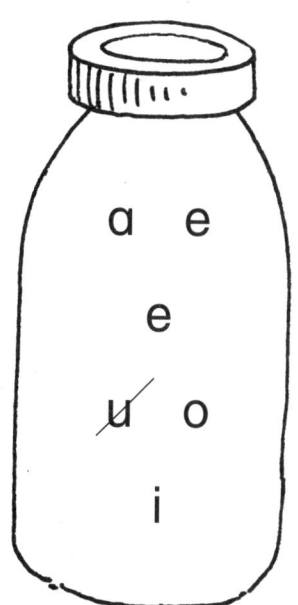
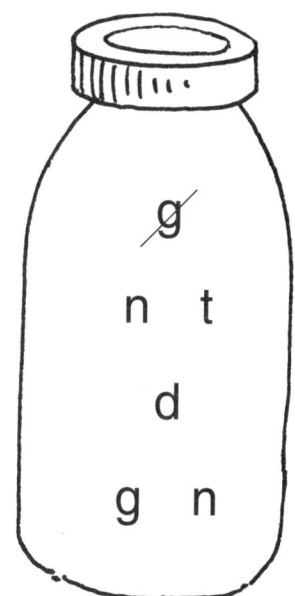

Use one letter from each jar to write the labels.

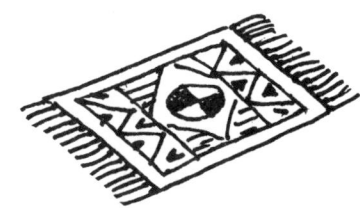

rug

8. Labels

Name: .... Date: ....

Start →	table	lamp	door	chair
door				lamp
chair				window
table				table
window				chair
lamp				window
door				door
window	table	lamp	chair	Go again

Teacher's Notes

Instructions:

1. Play in pairs. Each pair needs a dice. Each player needs a game sheet, coloured pencil and counter.
2. Take turns to throw the dice and move the number of squares.
3. When you land on a word, write it in the correct label, unless it has already been written there.
4. When all five labels are complete, check your partner's labels and spellings.
5. The winner is the player with most correct labels.

8. Labels

Name: ....   Date: ....

Copy each card.

Cut out the cards and play Picking up pairs.

scissors	paint
bricks	books
pencils	

Teacher's Notes

Instructions:

1. Once all 10 cards are complete, cut out.
2. In pairs, pupils turn their shuffled 20 cards face down.
3. Take it in turns to turn over two cards. If they are a pair, keep them. If not, replace them face down.
4. Continue until all cards have been picked up.
5. The winner is the player with the most cards. These cards can also be used for Snap.

   Y1T1: T12   **51**

Name: .... Date: ....

8. Labels

Copy the labels.

Cut them out to use in your classroom.

Name ....

This is my painting.

Name ....

This is my coat.

Name ....

Name ....

Teacher's Notes

These notices can be used for other labels, e.g. Please leave this model; I did this jig-saw; Please do not pack away.

9. Lists

Name: .... Date: ....

Draw arrows to the right pictures.

hats

crisps

balloons

drinks

Write the shopping list.
Draw arrows to the right pictures.

----

9. Lists

Name: .... Date: ....

Draw lines from the words to the right mask.

lion

tiger

parrot

monkey

Write the names of the animals on the list.

Draw lines from the masks to the right words.

Y1T1: W6/T15

9. Lists

Name: .... Date: ....

Cut out the pictures and put them in order.

Number the boxes in order.

Write the list on the lines below.

1. ....

2. ....

3. ....

4. ....

5. ....

Wilma and Biff run after the list.

Wilma is at the shops. She has a list.

The list blows away!

Anneena gets the list.

The list hits Wilf!

Name: .... Date: ....

Cut out the pictures and put them in order.

Number the boxes in order.

Write the list on the lines below.

1. ....

2. ....

3. ....

4. ....

5. ....

Lock Nora in the trap.

Get the key.

Get Wilma out.

Set a trap for Nora.

Get Nora to go in the trap.

Name: .... Date: ....

Cut out the pictures on the right hand side.

Choose which picture fits each letter.

Stick them in to finish Floppy's list.

A

B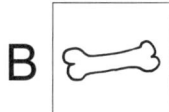

C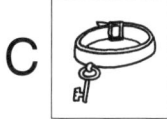

D

E

F

G

H

I

J

K

L

M

N

O

P

Q

R

S

T

U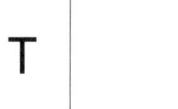

V

W

X

Y

Z

Name: .... Date: ....

Think of a word for each letter. It could be a friend's
name, a place you like, something you eat, a toy, etc.
Don't forget to use a capital letter for names.
Write the words in the spaces.

Aa ....   Jj ....   Ss ....

Bb ....   Kk ....   Tt ....

Cc ....   Ll ....   Uu ....

Dd ....   Mm ....   Vv ....

Ee ....   Nn ....   Ww ....

Ff ....   Oo ....   Xx ....

Gg ....   Pp ....   Yy ....

Hh ....   Qq ....   Zz ....

Ii ....   Rr ....

Name: .... **Date:** ....

Instructions:

1. Cut along the dotted lines.

2. Stick the Robark heads back to back.

3. Write 'Woof' in one speech bubble.

4. Write 'Foow' in the other speech bubble.

5. Take Robark home and tell the story.

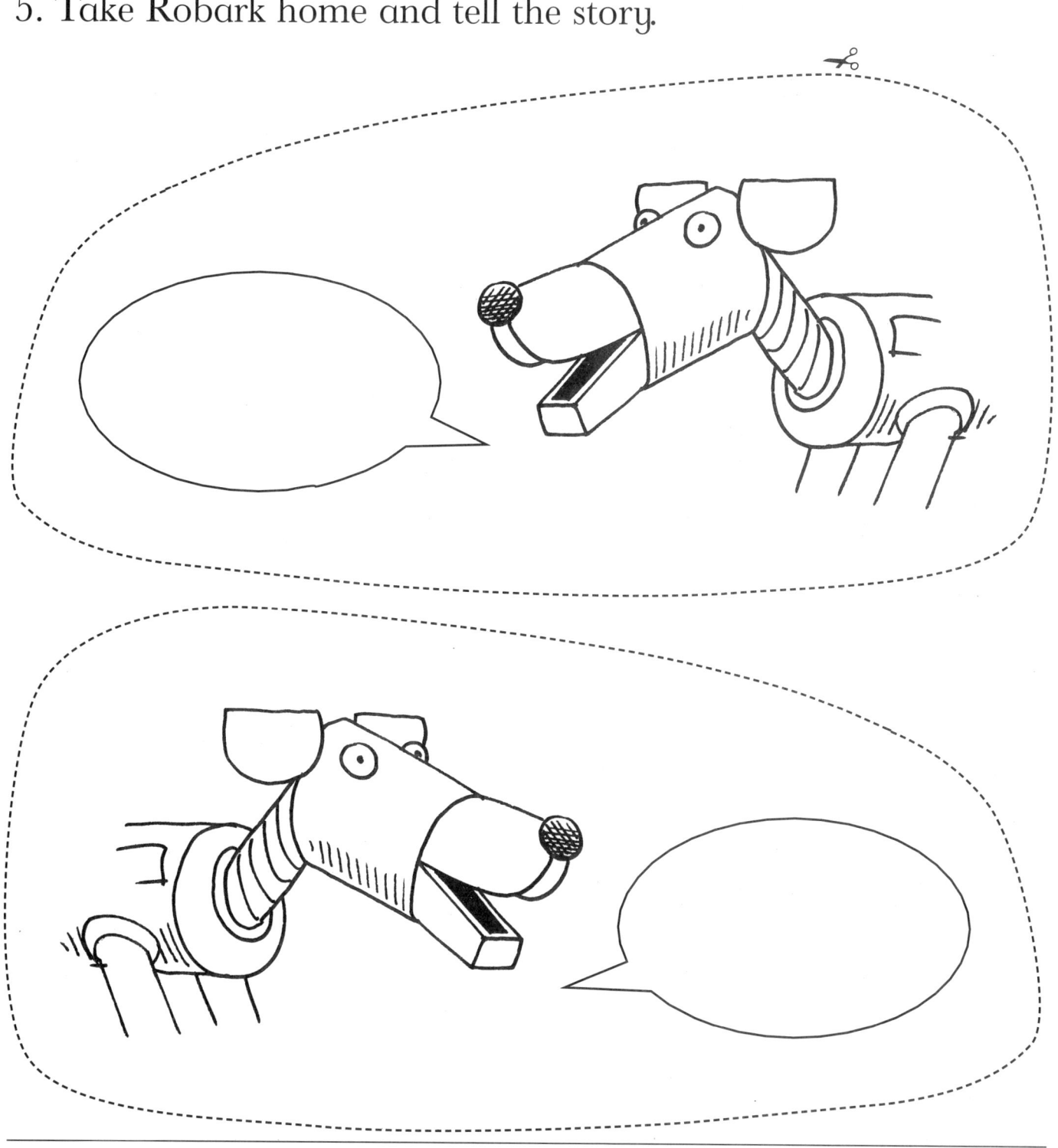

Name: .... Date: ....

Cut out the instructions.

Put them in order.

Getting up in the Morning.

1.

2.

3.

Go and wash.

Get out of bed.

Put on your clothes.

Teacher's Notes

Pupils can either cut out the instructions and paste them in the right order, or more able writers can copy the instructions in the right order and add small illustrations. If an adult helper is available, this is a good opportunity to use phonic cues for new words and to use the words 'first', 'next', 'after that', etc.

Name: .... Date: ....

Nadim made Wilf's robot. He

1. Put on the back legs.

2. Put on the front legs.

3. Put on the tail.

4. Put on the head.

Write the instructions to match the pictures.

1. Put on the head

2. Put on

3. Put

4.

Choose a notice to copy for your classroom.

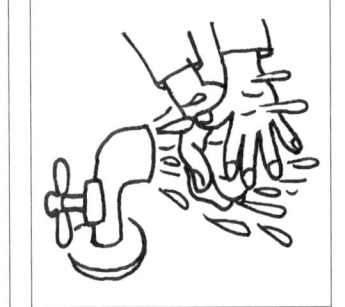

Please hang
up your coat.

Thank you.

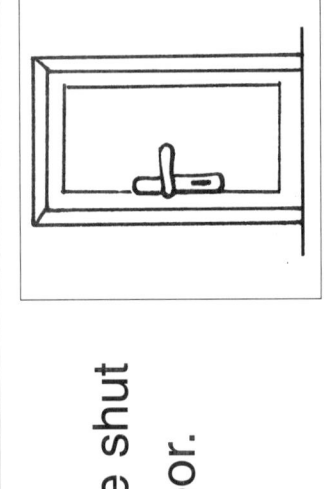

Please shut
the door.

Thank you.

Please wash
your hands.

Thank you.

Y1T1: T13/T16

10. Instructions

Name: .... Date: ....

Start	and	old	told	sent
bold	**Instructions**			hand
sold				fold
bent				land
sand				tent
hold				rent
cold	band	dent	sent	Go again

Instructions
1. Each player has a game sheet, a pencil, a counter and a dice to share.
2. Take turns to throw the dice and move along the track.
3. Write the word you land on in its rhyming set.
4. Go twice round the track.
5. The winner is the player who has written the most words in the right places.

gold

hand

tent

10. Instructions

Name: .... Date: ....

Write instructions for going out to play in winter.
Use these words.

coat	hat	gloves	scarf

put	on	do	up	your

Before you go out

1. ....

2. ....

3. ....

4. ....

Have fun!   Keep warm!